MY Dad builds AWESOME boats!

T0333856

Published in 2014 by
Speechmark Publishing Ltd, Sunningdale House, Caldecotte Lake Business Park,
Milton Keynes, MK7 8LF, UK
Tel: +44 (0) 1908 277177   Fax: +44 (0) 1908 278297
www.speechmark.net

002-5933/Printed in the United Kingdom by Hobbs the Printers.
British Library Cataloguing in Publication Data
A catalogue record for this book is available from the British Library

ISBN 978 0 86388 999 8

MY Dad builds

AWESOME boats!

Jo Johnson

Illustrated by Lauren Densham

NOTES FOR PARENTS

Parents who have a diagnosis of multiple sclerosis (MS) often ask "How can we talk to our children about MS?" The answer is straightforward: you can talk to them about MS in the same way that you talk to them about all other aspects of your lives as a family.

Honesty is vital. Children always know if things are being kept from them, and consequently imagine things to be much worse. They need to know that MS is a disease but that it is not something that can be caught or made worse by their behaviour.

Your child needs reassurance that it is not a terminal disease and they need to be given information about the most common symptoms.

They need an opportunity to ask questions and to feel that it is all right to ask questions at any time in the future. As they get older they will want more information as their cognitive ability improves.

It is my opinion that adults often overload children with too much information about the technical details of MS; the meaning of the name, why it causes the symptoms it does and how the brain and spinal cord are impaired. Some children like this kind of information but most simply want to know how it will impact them. Will mum still be able to take them to ballet or do the cooking? Can Dad still go swimming and kick a football?

This book has been designed so that children of between five and eight can read it independently. However, ideally it should be used with an adult to facilitate discussion about all aspects of family life and to enhance general emotional wellbeing. The book deliberately makes MS one of many things happening for this small group of children because for most children MS is only one of many issues in their family life.

The story is intended to emphasise that all families are different, with their own strengths and weaknesses and different experiences. MS is another experience that some people encounter and others do not.

Use the book as a template to enable you to create your own family book which is personal to your family life. Together, create a book that includes the names and adventures of your family and the positive and negative experiences that MS creates.

Jo Johnson

Consultant Neuropsychologist

Other books by the same author include:

"My Parent has a Brain Injury" ... a guide for young people
Aimed at older children and teenagers

In the Neurology Series:

My Dad makes the Best Boats
For younger children who have a Dad with a brain Injury

My Mum makes the Best cakes
For younger children who have a Mum with a brain Injury

My Mum bakes Awesome cakes!
For younger children who have a Mum with MS

Grandpa Seashells
Talking about Dementia

Everyone in Mrs Rutter's class is very excited. Tomorrow is the children's boat race at the village stream. The race happens just once a year. The winner is the first boat to get to the bridge.

"Who made the winning boat last year?" asks Mrs Rutter.

"Oscar won last year," says Samuel, "because his Dad makes great boats!"

Oscar smiles. He feels proud of his Dad.

"I wonder who will win this year," says Mrs Rutter.

What do you like making?

At bedtime Oscar and his Dad are reading a book together. Oscar's favourite book is about Rosie and Jim and their boat.

Dad and Oscar laugh at the picture of Rosie and Jim's boat crashing into the river bank.

"I hope my boat does not crash in the race", says Oscar.

"So do I," laughs Dad.

Oscar loves reading with his Dad.

What do you like doing with your Dad?

The boats are lined up ready to start the race.

All the Mums and Dads have come to watch. Mr Smart, the Head Teacher shouts, "Ready, steady…"

"…GO!" shout all the children.

What is your teacher's name?

Oscar and Samuel run along the edge of the stream to follow their boats.

"Hooray!" shouts Oscar, "my boat is the winner!"

Oscar's Dad gives him a hug. "We make a good team Oscar," he says.

"Your Dad makes great boats," says Samuel.

Samuel feels sad. "I wish my Dad would help me; my boat always sinks!"

"Next year," says Oscar, "My Dad will help you too."

What makes you feel sad?

The boys walk home with Oscar's Dad

"I like walking with your Dad," says Samuel. "He walks slowly like us. My Dad goes too fast and I get left behind."

Oscar's Dad smiles, "I have to walk slowly, I get tired."

Does your Dad get tired?

Today is sports day.

Samuel, Lauren and Oscar's team win the egg and spoon race. They are very excited.

Samuel's Dad runs in the Dads' race, but Oscar's Dad has MS so he can't run in the race. Oscar and his Dad cheer for Samuel's Dad and clap when he wins.

What things does your Dad find difficult?

The children go back into school.

"Why can't your Dad run?" asks Lauren.

"He has MS," Oscar says.

Lauren thinks he's said, "My Dad has a mess!" Oscar thinks that's funny.

The boys laugh; "Girls are so silly!"

Oscar tells his friends; "MS is a disease that makes my Dad's legs go wobbly and makes him tired and sometimes a bit grumpy."

Do you talk to your friends about MS?

After school Oscar and his friends are at running club.

"Why don't you have wobbly legs like your Dad?"
Lauren asks.

Oscar laughs; "You can't catch MS or get it from your
Dad; it is not like a cold or chicken pox!"

The boys think girls are very silly. Samuel wishes he
could run as fast as Oscar.

can you run fast?

Oscar is eating his dinner. It's his favourite; chicken nuggets and chips.

Dad is upstairs injecting the medicine he takes for MS. "Mum?" Oscar says, "At school I told Lauren that you can't catch MS."

"That's right," Mum answers.

"But if you can't catch it, how did Dad get MS?"

What is your favourite food?

"That is a good question but nobody really knows why some people get it."

Dad says, "The good thing is that lots of doctors are working very hard to find out why some people get MS so they can help people like me."

"I hope they find out soon," says Oscar.

"Me too," says Dad.

Do you have any questions about MS?

Samuel is having tea with his mum. He is sad. He is worried that Oscar's Dad might die. Samuel's Mum smiles and gives him a hug.

"MS does not kill people Samuel, it just makes some things difficult," she says. "Oscar's Dad gets more tired than other Dads. Some of the time it is difficult for him to walk and sometimes his eyes go funny and he can't drive."

Samuel feels happy that Oscar's Dad can keep making great boats.

What makes you feel worried?

Mum is cross. Oscar's sister Katie has got paint on the chair.

Mum shouts at Katie.

Katie cries and Dad tries to pick her up.

Dad's legs go wobbly and he has to put Katie back down.

Do your Dad's legs go wobbly sometimes?

Oscar shouts at his sister. "You have made Dad's MS bad by being so naughty!"

Mum says, "Nobody can make Dad's MS bad or good. Dad is having a bad day because of the MS, not because we have all been grumpy."

Dad brings out some of Mum's homemade cake. They all eat it and everyone feels happy again.

What makes you feel happy?

Today is Father's Day. Mrs Rutter asks the children about their Dads.

Oscar and Samuel like Mrs Rutter; she is kind. The teacher gives them all a piece of card cut into the shape of a car.

"Write something nice about your Dad," says Mrs Rutter.

Do you have a favourite teacher?

Samuel writes "My Dad runs fast."

Lauren writes "My Dad reads me stories; I love stories."

Oscar writes "My Dad makes great boats."

They all stick their pictures on a big poster. The poster says "Our Dads are great".

Write something nice about your Dad.

Tomorrow is the children's boat race.

Oscar's Dad is helping Oscar and Samuel to finish their boats.

Oscar's Dad says "Samuel, don't forget to put on the sail; we want your boat to go faster than it did last year!"

Why don't you try and build a boat?

The race is nearly over and Oscar and Samuel are waiting at the bridge to see which boat is going to win.

"It's a draw!" shouts Mrs Rutter. Samuel and Oscar are both the winners.

"Our boats got to the bridge at the same time," Oscar tells his Dad.

"Thank you, you make great boats!" Samuel says to Oscar's Dad.

"I think so too," laughs Oscar.

Who is your best friend?

My Dad builds
AWESOME
boats!

Activity pages

Spot the Difference

Can you spot the 11 differences?

Wordsearch

B	S	W	F	Z	N	A	U	S	L	C	G	M	P	M
A	E	S	V	A	I	U	P	K	J	Y	N	O	L	U
L	I	T	E	X	T	A	R	R	Y	N	I	O	A	S
A	F	R	A	N	S	I	M	S	E	B	R	D	T	C
N	F	T	K	M	B	Y	G	U	E	X	R	S	J	U
C	A	G	G	U	E	M	R	U	G	B	U	S	S	L
E	E	N	K	L	H	O	U	E	E	R	L	G	J	O
B	R	A	I	N	L	U	K	N	L	V	B	E	T	S
M	X	N	N	O	R	U	E	N	G	C	M	L	Y	K
S	E	A	G	E	V	R	E	N	G	C	S	Y	R	E
O	E	I	S	S	E	N	I	Z	Z	I	D	U	O	L
P	S	Y	N	L	V	K	M	V	Y	I	L	V	M	E
T	H	J	E	F	L	V	E	R	T	I	G	O	E	T
B	G	X	V	A	Z	R	F	D	L	K	C	S	M	A
J	X	B	W	T	T	O	A	J	T	A	A	C	J	L

ataxia	legs	neurologist
balance	memory	neuron
blurring	moods	numbness
brain	muscle	nurse
dizziness	musculoskeletal	spasm
eyes	myelin	vertigo
fatigue	nerve	walking

21

All about me...

My Name is

These are the people in
my family

Draw your favourite food on
the plate below

I don't like

Colour the shape below in your
favourite colour

The colour of my eyes is

Draw your house in the
cloud below

Draw a picture of your family

All about my Dad...

Here are some facts about
my Dad...

Draw a picture of your Dad doing
his favourite thing in
the box below

Name ....

Hair colour ....

Eye colour ....

Birthday ....

Favourite animal ....

Favourite sport ....

He really doesn't like...

Think of something you could do
to make your Dad smile and
write it in the cloud below

Does your Dad have a favourite
thing he often says? Write it in
the speech bubble below!

Spot the Difference
Answers

1 Mrs "Putters Class" written on board

2 Clock hand shortened

3 10M boat measurement not 10cm

4 Orange not yellow sun on drawing on wall

5 Mrs Rutter has pink bead on necklace

6 Holly has no lips!

7 Georgina's hair bobble is a different colour

8 Name on boat on poster "Jolly Doger"

9 Reward Chart extra red face .

10 "Fridad!" instead of "Friday" on reward chart

11 Left top Drawing pin on poster coloured black

For further information and support on
Multiple Sclerosis, please visit the websites below:

www.mstrust.org.uk

www.shift.ms

www.mssociety.org.uk